7/03

Dr. Seuss

My Favorite Writer

Jill Foran

WEIGL PUBLISHERS INC.

Published by Weigl Publishers Inc.
123 South Broad Street, Box 227
Mankato, MN 56002
USA
Web site: www.weigl.com

Library of Congress Cataloging-in-Publication Data

Foran, Jill.
  Theodore Seuss Geisel / Jill Foran.
      p. cm. -- (My favorite writer)
Summary: A biography of American author Dr. Seuss, whose first published book was "And To Think That I Saw It On Mulberry Street," plus a chapter of creative writing tips.
  ISBN 1-59036-028-1 (lib. bdg. : alk. paper)
 1. Seuss, Dr.--Juvenile literature. 2. Authors, American--20th century--Biography--Juvenile literature. 3. Illustrators--United States--Biography--Juvenile literature. 4. Children's literature--Authorship--Juvenile literature. [1. Seuss, Dr. 2. Authors, American. 3. Illustrators. 4. Authorship.] I. Title. II. Series.
  PS3513.E2 Z67 2002
  813'.52--dc21

                                        2002005586

Printed in Canada
1 2 3 4 5 6 7 8 9 10 06 05 04 03 02

Editor
Jennifer Nault

Copy Editor
Heather Kissock

Design and Layout
Terry Paulhus

Photo Researcher
Tina Schwartzenberger

Contents

Dr. Seuss

MILESTONES

1904 Theodor Seuss Geisel is born in Springfield, Massachusetts on March 2

1925 Graduates from Dartmouth College with a degree in English

1927 Sells a cartoon to the *Saturday Evening Post* and marries Helen Palmer

1937 *And to Think That I Saw It on Mulberry Street* is published

1957 *The Cat in the Hat* is published

1967 Wife, Helen, dies on October 23

1984 Wins a Pulitzer Prize for his great contribution to children's **literature**

1991 Dies in La Jolla, California on September 24 at the age of 87

Few children's writers are as well known and admired as Dr. Seuss. For more than fifty years, he wrote and illustrated wonderful children's books. Today, these books are still read and enjoyed by people of all ages. Dr. Seuss's imaginative stories are brought to life with his brightly colored illustrations. People around the world recognize Dr. Seuss's characters. The Cat in the Hat, the Grinch, and Horton the elephant are just a few of the characters found in his popular children's books. Dr. Seuss's books are written in a **rhythmic**, rhyming **verse** that makes readers laugh out loud in delight. He has shown children and adults around the world that reading is great fun.

Dr. Seuss claimed that the reason he wrote so well for children was because he never grew up himself. He often said that everything he wrote or illustrated was created for his own amusement. His work continues to amuse millions of readers all over the world. Dr. Seuss's stories are timeless.

Early Childhood

D r. Seuss was born Theodor Seuss Geisel on March 2, 1904. He was named after his father, Theodor Robert. From the time Dr. Seuss was young, his family and friends called him Ted. Ted grew up in the town of Springfield, Massachusetts. His father was a kind man who worked in a **brewery** for many years. Ted's mother, Henrietta, worked in a bakery. She also took care of Ted, his older sister Marnie, and his younger sister, Henrietta. Both parents were of German **descent**, and their children grew up speaking German and English.

The Geisels were a close family, and they had many happy times together. They also experienced some hardships. When Ted was 3 years old, his youngest sister, Henrietta, died of **pneumonia**. The entire family mourned the loss.

When Ted was a little boy, he would fall asleep every night listening to his mother recite poems. She made them up for customers while working in the bakery each day. They were rhymes about different pie flavors. The poems had a fast, catchy rhythm that Ted really liked.

■ Dr. Seuss's birthplace, Springfield, Massachusetts, is surrounded by five New England states: Maine, New Hampshire, Vermont, Connecticut, and Rhode Island.

Theodor and Henrietta encouraged their children to read. They would often bring Ted and Marnie to the local library. Ted would check out as many books as he could carry. He loved to read, and before he was even 10 years old, he was reading books that were written for adults.

Along with reading, Ted also loved to draw. He would spend hours at the Springfield Zoo, watching the different animals. Then he would go home and draw the animals he had seen. But Ted's animals never looked much like those at the zoo. He was not content to just copy them. He had to make them look original. Ted's animals were **bizarre** copies of the real ones, and he gave them equally bizarre names. Henrietta was very proud of her son's artwork, and she encouraged him to keep drawing. She even let him draw on the attic walls.

■ When he was a young boy, Ted would study the animals at the Springfield Zoo for hours. The character Horton the elephant was inspired by the elephants Ted watched at the zoo.

Growing Up

Ted was well liked by his peers when he was growing up, but there was a difficult period during his youth when he was bullied at school. In 1914, World War I began. In the United States, people of German descent were judged harshly. Some people in Springfield insulted the Geisels because the family was of German background. During this period, Ted was unfairly mocked at school. This confused him, and often made him feel very lonely.

Ted worked hard to rise above the taunts of his schoolmates. He was shy, but he was also very funny. In 1917, he entered Springfield's Central High School. Ted began to write and draw for the school newspaper. He also acted in a few school plays. It did not take long for Ted to become known for his humor and creativity.

In his last year of high school, Ted was voted Class Wit and Class Artist.

8

Ted's years at Springfield's Central High School were busy ones. Although his father wanted him to join the school's sports teams, Ted was much more interested in working for the newspaper. It was called the *Central Recorder*. He often wrote funny one-line **quips** known as "grinds." He also contributed poems, **satires**, and cartoons to the *Central Recorder*. The school paper included so much of Ted's work that he often had to use a **pseudonym**. His pseudonym was T. S. LeSieg. The last name was "Geisel" spelled backward.

Ted received good grades throughout high school. One of his favorite subjects was English. This was partly because he had an English teacher who inspired him. The teacher's name was Edwin A. "Red" Smith. Ted once said that it was Red Smith who **motivated** him to write. Before long, it was time for Ted to decide where he should go to college. He chose to go to Dartmouth College in Hanover, New Hampshire because that was where Red had gone.

Inspired to Write

Even as a child, Ted looked at things from his own unique **perspective**. This often gave him the inspiration to write and illustrate. He had to put his imaginative ideas on paper. Ted believed in looking at life through the wrong end of the telescope. He thought that this would bring forth new and exciting ideas.

After he graduated from high school, Ted attended Dartmouth College. Today, the college holds a yearly "green eggs and ham" feast in his honor.

Ted began classes at Dartmouth College in the fall of 1921. He **majored** in English, but his true interest in college was Dartmouth's humor magazine, the *Jack-O-Lantern*. Ted discovered the magazine soon after he arrived at Dartmouth. Almost immediately, he began contributing cartoons. He made many good friends at the magazine. The college students admired his work and thought he was funny. By the end of his junior year, Ted was elected editor of the *Jack-O-Lantern*. He had worked toward this position since he arrived at Dartmouth College.

Ted was a good editor, but he did not keep the position for very long. During his last year at Dartmouth, he and some friends were caught breaking a school rule. As punishment, the position of editor was taken away from Ted. Of course, this did not stop him from working for the magazine. He still contributed many articles, only now he used pseudonyms instead of his real name. It was at that time that Ted first began using the name "Seuss," which was his mother's maiden name. It was also during this time that Ted recognized the power of joining words and pictures.

Favorite Authors

Growing up, Ted loved to read all kinds of literature. Every evening, his father came home from work with the daily newspaper. Ted would flip through it, looking for the comics. He read the jokes and studied the drawings. Ted also enjoyed reading books and poetry. One of his favorite book series was called *The Rover Boys*. He once read thirty of these books in a row. When he was a little older, Ted discovered a book called *The Bad Child's Book of Beasts*, written by Hilaire Belloc. This book was made up of a series of poems about naughty children. The rhymes and rhythms of these funny poems impressed Ted.

While at Dartmouth, Ted was so busy with the *Jack-O-Lantern* that he had little time left over for his regular classes. There was only one class that really held his interest. It was a creative writing course taught by a man named Ben Pressey. Ben was very supportive of Ted's writing. He inspired Ted in college the same way that Red Smith had in high school.

After Ted graduated from Dartmouth, he still had no idea what he wanted to do for a living. In the fall of 1925, he moved to England to attend Oxford University. While there, he met and fell in love with a fellow student named Helen Palmer. Although he and Helen were very happy together, Ted could not find happiness in his studies. He spent more time doodling in his notebook than he did listening to his professors. Helen admired Ted's doodles and drawings. She helped convince Ted that he should try illustrating for a living. Ted left Oxford to pursue new goals.

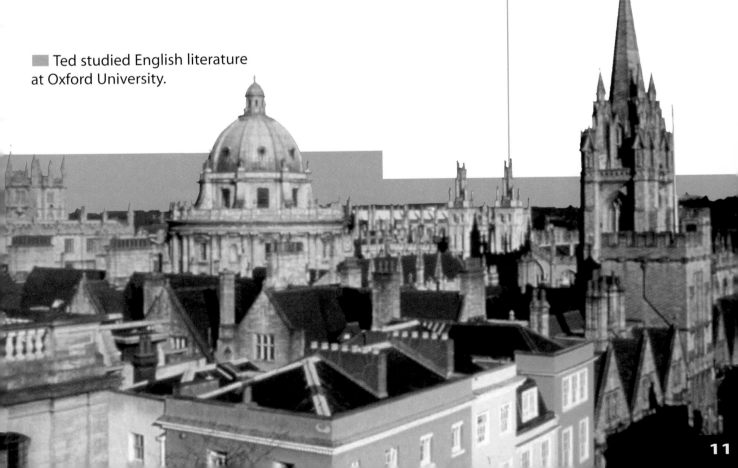

Ted studied English literature at Oxford University.

Learning the Craft

Every day, Ted sat at his father's desk and drew. He sent his drawings out to all of the popular magazines.

After leaving Oxford University, Ted spent some time traveling around Europe. He toured parts of Austria, Italy, and France, and lived for a short time in Paris. In February 1927, he returned to the United States and moved back into his parents' house in Springfield. At the time, Ted did not have a job. However, he had a clear goal. He wanted to get his cartoons published.

Every day, Ted sat at his father's desk and drew. He sent his drawings out to popular magazines. After many rejections, a magazine called the *Saturday Evening Post* bought one of his cartoons for $25. Soon after that success, Ted moved to New York. He showed his drawings to the editor of a magazine called *Judge* and was quickly hired as a writer and artist. In November 1927, Ted married his sweetheart from university, Helen Palmer.

Ted worked very hard at *Judge*. He drew funny cartoons, and wrote short, humorous essays. Most of these contributions were given the **byline**, "Seuss." It was also during his time at *Judge* that Ted added the title "Dr." to his name. He claimed that the name "Dr. Seuss" made him seem more **credible**.

Ted submitted cartoons to the *Saturday Evening Post, Life, Vanity Fair,* and *Liberty* magazines.

Ted's work at *Judge* led to one of the luckiest breaks of his life. He drew a cartoon that featured a knight in bed with a dragon nuzzling him. The **caption** beneath the cartoon read, "Darn it all, another dragon. And just after I'd sprayed the whole castle with Flit." Flit was an **insecticide** that people used to kill insects. When the owners of Flit saw the cartoon, they were impressed. The cartoon led to a contract for Ted to write all of Flit's advertisements. These ads became famous.

Despite his success in advertising, Ted wanted to work on other projects. He was hired to illustrate a book called *Boners*, which was published in 1931. The book was very popular, and Ted's drawings received great reviews. However, Ted did not receive any **royalties** from the sales. As an artist, he had been paid a **flat fee** for his work. Ted decided that if he wanted to make a living, he would have to write as well as draw.

Inspired to Write

Throughout his career, Ted loved to be challenged. In the late 1950s, Ted's editor bet him $50 that he could not write a book using just 100 different words. Ted insisted that he could do even better than that. He boasted that he could write a book using just fifty different words! Ted won the bet a few months later when he completed *Green Eggs and Ham*.

Ted decided to start writing books for children when he was about 30 years old.

Getting Published

The first book that Ted wrote and illustrated was a children's alphabet book. It was filled with his colorful, imaginative drawings. He sent his new **manuscript** to several publishers in the United States, but not one of these companies was interested in publishing it. After these rejections, Ted decided to forget about his children's book. He went back to his work in advertising.

Ted did not attempt to write a book again until 1936. That year, he toured Europe with Helen. They returned home on a ship, sailing from France to New York. During the journey, Ted could not stop listening to the rhythm of the ship's engines. After a while, he began making up silly words and rhymes to go along with the whirring sound. He soon found himself chanting the words, "And that is a story that no one can beat; and to think that I saw it on Mulberry Street." Ted decided that he needed to write and illustrate a story to go along with these words.

> "I know my stuff all looks like it was rattled off in twenty-three seconds, but every word is a struggle."
> Dr. Seuss

The Publishing Process

Publishing companies receive hundreds of manuscripts from authors each year. Only a few manuscripts become books. Publishers must be sure that a manuscript will sell many copies. As a result, publishers reject most of the manuscripts they receive.

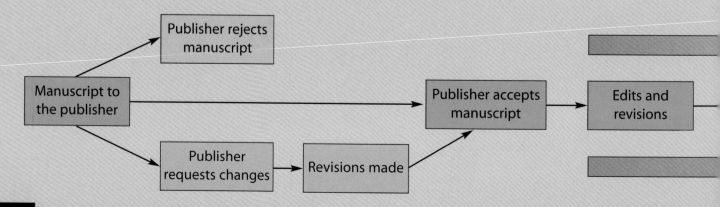

It took Ted six months to write and illustrate the book. When he was finished, he presented it to about thirty different publishers. It was rejected by all of them. They told Ted that the book would not sell because it was too different.

After yet another unsuccessful meeting with a publisher, Ted became very discouraged. He decided to take his book home and burn it. As he trudged back to his apartment, Ted bumped into an old friend from Dartmouth College named Mike McClintock. Ted told him about the book. Mike, an editor for Vanguard Press, asked him if he could read the book. Within one hour, Ted had signed a contract to have his first book published.

The book was titled *And to Think That I Saw It on Mulberry Street*. Published under the name "Dr. Seuss" in 1937, it quickly became a bestseller. Over the next three years, Dr. Seuss produced three more children's books: *The 500 Hats of Bartholomew Cubbins*, *The King's Stilts*, and *Horton Hatches the Egg*.

Once a manuscript has been accepted, it goes through many stages before it is published. Often, authors change their work to follow an editor's suggestions. Once the book is published, some authors receive royalties. This is money based on book sales.

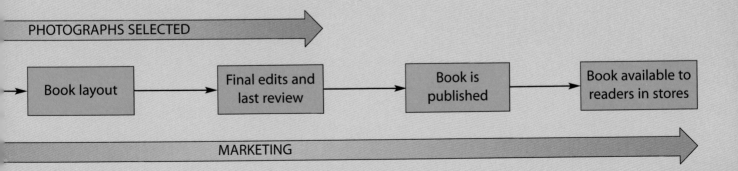

PHOTOGRAPHS SELECTED

Book layout → Final edits and last review → Book is published → Book available to readers in stores

MARKETING

Writer Today

Ted and Helen Geisel moved to La Jolla, California in 1948. Ted lived and worked there for the rest of his life. The Seuss's property in La Jolla was the highest point in the area. It was also the location of an abandoned observation tower, which stood overlooking the Pacific Ocean. Ted and Helen built a pink stucco house around the tower, and Ted converted the tower room into an office.

Although Ted never had children of his own, he connected with children around the globe through his books. Sadly, in 1967, Helen Geisel passed away. Shortly after, Ted married Audrey Diamond, a longtime friend.

In 1984, Dr. Seuss was awarded a Pulitzer Prize for his special contribution to children's literature. He was honored for his work, which spanned fifty years.

As he grew older, Dr. Seuss continued to produce bestsellers, despite his failing health. He did not want to retire. Ted was not ready to give up the joys of writing and illustrating. In 1990, Dr. Seuss came out with a book called *Oh, the Places You'll Go*. The book was on the *New York Times* bestseller list longer than any other children's book. Unfortunately, it was Ted's last book.

Ted and Helen purchased an old observation tower in La Jolla, California. It was in this tower that Dr. Seuss wrote and illustrated most of his books.

On September 24, 1991, Ted passed away in his sleep. His death was mourned by devoted fans, young and old, around the world. Along with his books, Ted's **legacy** includes a charitable fund called the Dr. Seuss Foundation. Today, the foundation continues to contribute money and resources to libraries, charities, and zoos.

Ted Geisel dedicated much of his career to making reading fun. He made a major contribution to reading and children's literature. Today, schools across the United States hold a "Read Across America" day each year on his birthday. On this day, students, teachers, and other members of the community share books and enjoy reading circles.

Popular Books

Dr. Seuss had a long and successful writing career. Although most of his books were written for children, adults love his stories, too. Today, many parents who read Dr. Seuss books with their children can remember reading the same books when they were young. The following are some of Dr. Seuss's best-loved books:

And to Think That I Saw It on Mulberry Street

Dr. Seuss's first book tells the story of Marco, a young boy with a wonderful imagination. Every day, Marco's father asks him what he has seen on the way to and from school. Marco tells his father imaginative stories, but his father gets impatient and tells Marco not to tell tales. One afternoon, while Marco is walking along Mulberry Street, he sees a horse and a wagon. These are not exciting sights to young Marco, so he imagines different sights instead. Before long, a wonderful, imaginary parade is marching down Mulberry Street. When Marco returns home, his father asks him what he has seen. What Marco decides to tell his father will amuse and surprise readers.

Horton Hatches the Egg

Horton Hatches the Egg is a touching story about the rewards of keeping a promise. The story begins when a lazy bird named Mayzie becomes tired of sitting on her egg. She spots a kind elephant named Horton and begs him to sit on her nest while she is away on vacation. Horton agrees to sit up in the tree on Mayzie's nest. He sits and sits, but Mayzie does not return. Horton endures many challenges while sitting in the tree. Still, he never leaves the nest because of his promise to Mayzie. When the egg finally hatches, no one is more surprised than Horton at what pops out.

McElligot's Pool

This book is about imagination, patience, and hope. The main character of the tale is Marco, who was also the hero in *And to Think That I Saw It on Mulberry Street*. This time, Marco is trying to fish at McElligot's Pool, but he is told that he will not catch anything because the pool is full of junk. Marco imagines that McElligot's Pool winds its way under farms and villages and connects to the sea. He pictures different kinds of fascinating fish swimming in the pool.

AWARDS
McElligot's Pool

1947 Caldecott Honor Award
1950 Young Reader's Choice Award

How the Grinch Stole Christmas!

This story is enjoyed by many children during the Christmas season. A grumpy creature named the Grinch lives on top of Mount Crumpet, high above the town of Whoville. The Grinch dislikes just about everything, but he especially dislikes Christmas. He cannot stand the presents, feasting, singing, and noise. He has put up with Christmas for too many years. This year, he decides to put an end to all the Christmas cheer in Whoville. On Christmas Eve, the Grinch steals every present, treat, and decoration in town. He is certain that everyone in Whoville will be devastated. However, when Christmas Day arrives, the Grinch is greeted by a surprise that changes him for the better.

How the Grinch Stole Christmas! was made into a television movie special in 1966.

The Cat in the Hat

When two children find themselves at home alone on a rainy day, the Cat in the Hat comes to play. The children are bored because they cannot go outside. Suddenly, a cat in a tall hat comes through the front door, bringing all kinds of excitement. The children watch, amazed, as the Cat in the Hat and his friends make a terrible mess of the house. How will they clean up the mess before their mother comes home?

Green Eggs and Ham

The funny book, *Green Eggs and Ham*, was written for early readers. The story follows a pesky character named Sam-I-Am. He is trying to get another character in the book to eat green eggs and ham. Although the other character says that he cannot stand the meal, Sam-I-Am keeps bothering him until he finally agrees to taste it. What happens next will be a great surprise to readers.

The Lorax

This book is about the dangers of greed and **environmental** destruction. The story begins when a beast called a Once-ler discovers a beautiful forest. The forest is filled with happy animals, fresh water, and countless Truffula trees. These beautiful trees have tufts that are softer than silk. The Once-ler decides to use the tufts to knit something called a Thneed. He knows he can sell the Thneed and become rich. When the Once-ler chops down a Truffula tree, a short, brown creature pops out of the stump. The creature is called the Lorax, and he speaks for the trees. The Lorax asks the Once-ler not to cut down any more Truffulas, but the Once-ler ignores his pleas. Soon, the entire forest is in danger.

Creative Writing Tips

Writing a story or a poem can be challenging, but it can also be very rewarding. Some writers have trouble coming up with ideas, while others have so many ideas that they do not know where to start. The writing process can be slow at times, but the results are worth it. Dr. Seuss had special writing habits that young writers can follow to develop their ideas into great stories.

Keep Your Eyes and Ears Open

Many writers get ideas by watching people and listening to conversations. If you pay attention, you will see that most people say and do all sorts of interesting things. These things can inspire writers to develop characters or to write funny scenes. Dr. Seuss found a great deal of inspiration in conversations or things he overheard. He would use his own imagination to make them more amusing.

Dr. Seuss found a great deal of inspiration in conversations or things he overheard.

Write, Write, Write

Sometimes, the easiest way to finish a poem or a story is to write as much as possible in a first **draft**. This way, a writer can get all of his or her ideas down on paper. Then, the writer can decide which parts to keep. Very few writers have ever produced a great story in just one draft. Instead, they may review their first draft to see which parts should stay and what needs to be **revised**. Dr. Seuss claimed that the secret to his success was writing too much. He would often write and draw more than 500 pages of material for a 60-page book.

The Creative Process

Most writers have different opinions about when is the best time to write. Some work best late at night when everyone else is asleep. Others claim that they are most productive early in the morning. There are also differing approaches to the writing process. Some writers need to make a detailed outline. This is a good idea for new writers, as it will help them to organize their thoughts. Some writers do not use an outline; they simply begin writing and let their ideas flow. Dr. Seuss had no set pattern to his creative process. Sometimes, he would write and illustrate a book all at once. Other times, he would write a story and add the illustrations later.

It Takes Dedication

Writing takes dedication and discipline. Dr. Seuss spent at least 8 hours per day working on his stories and illustrations. It was this dedication, along with his ability to make work fun, which led to so many successful books.

Dr. Seuss claimed that many of his books started as scribbles and doodles.

Writing a Biography Review

A biography is an account of an individual's life that is written by another person. Some people's lives are very interesting. In school, you may be asked to write a biography review. The first thing to do when writing a biography review is to decide whom you would like to learn about. Your school library or community library will have a large selection of biographies from which to choose.

Are you interested in an author, a sports figure, an inventor, a movie star, or a president? Finding the right book is your first task. Whether you choose to write your review on a biography of Dr. Seuss or another person, the task will be similar.

Begin your review by writing the title of the book, the author, and the person featured in the book. Then, start writing about the main events in the person's life. Include such things as where the person grew up and what his or her childhood was like. You will want to add details about the person's adult life, such as whether he or she married or had children. Next, write about what you think makes this person special. What kinds of experiences influenced this individual? For instance, did he or she grow up in unusual circumstances? Was the person determined to accomplish a goal? Include any details that surprised you.

A concept web is a useful research tool. Use the concept web on the right to begin researching your biography review.

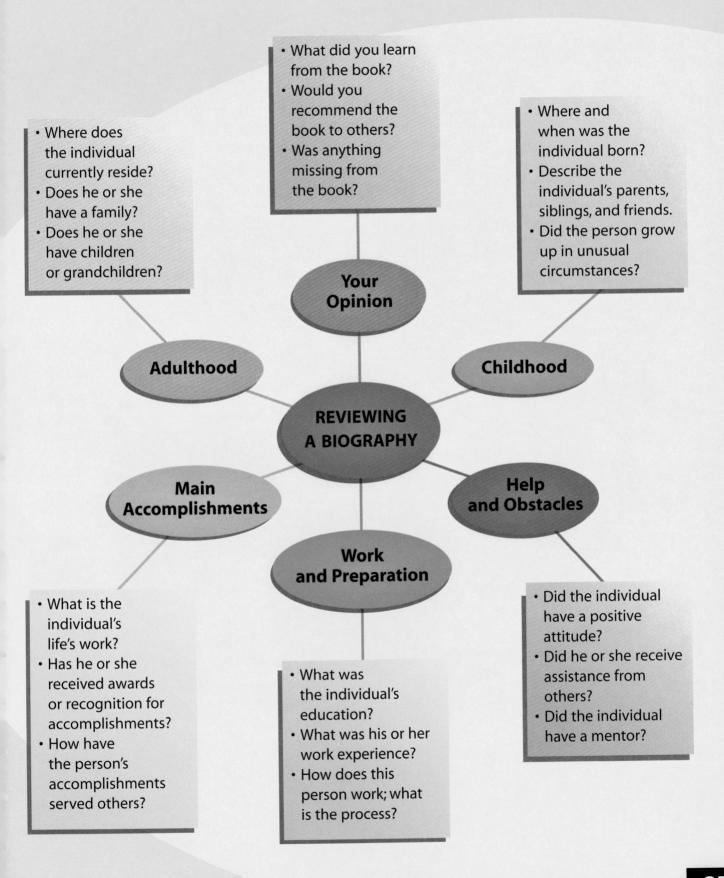

• What did you learn from the book?
• Would you recommend the book to others?
• Was anything missing from the book?

• Where and when was the individual born?
• Describe the individual's parents, siblings, and friends.
• Did the person grow up in unusual circumstances?

• Where does the individual currently reside?
• Does he or she have a family?
• Does he or she have children or grandchildren?

Your Opinion

Adulthood

Childhood

REVIEWING A BIOGRAPHY

Main Accomplishments

Help and Obstacles

Work and Preparation

• What is the individual's life's work?
• Has he or she received awards or recognition for accomplishments?
• How have the person's accomplishments served others?

• What was the individual's education?
• What was his or her work experience?
• How does this person work; what is the process?

• Did the individual have a positive attitude?
• Did he or she receive assistance from others?
• Did the individual have a mentor?

Fan Information

How the Grinch Stole *Christmas!* was made into a feature film in 2000.

For more than fifty years, Dr. Seuss wrote wonderful books that made reading fun. He has millions of dedicated fans. Throughout his career, Ted received great quantities of fan mail. As early as 1957, he was receiving more than 9,000 pounds of fan mail each year. Ted was sent letters of gratitude, valentines, drawings, and countless birthday cards. After he published *Green Eggs and Ham* in 1960, Ted began receiving strange packages. People began sending him green eggs and ham!

Ted was always busy. He usually did not have the time to respond to most of his mail. Still, Ted did attend many book signings. Once in a while, he made appearances at schools and special events. He was also known for welcoming curious fans into his home in La Jolla.

Today, more than 200 million copies of Dr. Seuss's books have been sold. They have been translated into more than twenty different languages, and have been turned into television specials and feature films.

Many fans have created impressive Web sites to share information about Dr. Seuss. To find Web sites on Dr. Seuss and his inspiring life and work, type "Dr. Seuss" or "Theodor Seuss Geisel" into a search engine such as Google or Yahoo.

WEB LINKS

Seussville
www.randomhouse.com/seussville
This is a great Web site for fans of Dr. Seuss to visit. Be careful, you may never want to leave! The Seussville Web site offers games, recent events, music, and much, much more.

ESeuss
www.eseuss.com
Along with plenty of information, ESeuss offers games, trivia, and puzzles on the life and work of Dr. Seuss.

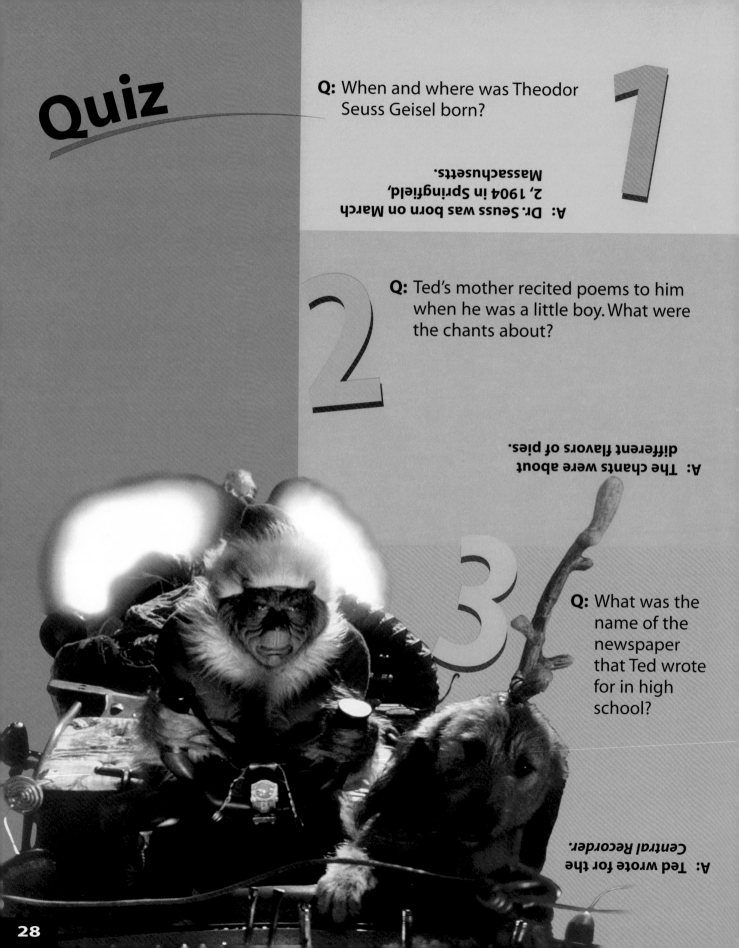

Quiz

Q: When and where was Theodor Seuss Geisel born?

1

A: Dr. Seuss was born on March 2, 1904 in Springfield, Massachusetts.

2

Q: Ted's mother recited poems to him when he was a little boy. What were the chants about?

A: The chants were about different flavors of pies.

3

Q: What was the name of the newspaper that Ted wrote for in high school?

A: Ted wrote for the *Central Recorder*.

Q: What was Ted's pseudonym for the *Central Recorder*?

A: Ted's pseudonym was T. S. LeSieg, "Geisel" spelled backward.

Q: What college did Ted attend in the United States?

A: Dartmouth College

Q: For what product was Ted contracted to write and illustrate advertisements?

A: Flit Insecticide

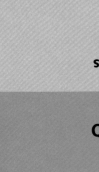

Q: With whom did Ted meet and fall in love while he was in England?

A: Helen Palmer

Q: What was Ted's first published children's book?

A: *And to Think That I Saw It on Mulberry Street*

Q: Where did Dr. Seuss live and work for most of his adult life?

A: La Jolla, California

Q: How many Dr. Seuss books have been sold over the years?

A: More than 200 million books have been sold.

Writing Terms

This glossary will introduce you to some of the main terms in the field of writing. Understanding these common writing terms will allow you to discuss your ideas about books and writing with others.

action: the moving events of a work of fiction

antagonist: the person in the story who opposes the main character

autobiography: a history of a person's life written by that person

biography: a written account of another person's life

character: a person in a story, poem, or play

climax: the most exciting moment or turning point in a story

episode: a short piece of action, or scene, in a story

fiction: stories about characters and events that are not real

foreshadow: hinting at something that is going to happen later in the book

imagery: a written description of a thing or idea that brings an image to mind

narrator: the speaker of the story who relates the events

nonfiction: writing that deals with real people and events

novel: published writing of considerable length that portrays characters within a story

plot: the order of events in a work of fiction

protagonist: the leading character of a story; often a likable character

resolution: the end of the story, when the conflict is settled

scene: a single episode in a story

setting: the place and time in which a work of fiction occurs

theme: an idea that runs throughout a work of fiction

Glossary

bizarre: odd or unusual

brewery: a place where beer is made

byline: a printed line beneath the title of a piece of writing that gives the author's name

caption: a short piece of writing that describes or explains an illustration

credible: trustworthy, reliable

descent: family background

draft: a rough copy of a story

environmental: relating to the natural world

flat fee: a fixed amount of money paid for a story

insecticide: a substance used for killing insects

legacy: something handed down

literature: writing of lasting value, including plays, poems, and novels

majored: a student's main field of study

manuscript: a draft of a story before it is published

motivated: provided with the eagerness to do something

perspective: one person's mental view of facts and ideas

pneumonia: an illness characterized by an inflammation of the lungs

pseudonym: a fictitious name used by an author; a pen name

quips: short, clever remarks

revised: amended; changed

rhythmic: having a patterned beat or rhythm

royalties: payments made to an author based on sales of his or her work

satires: stories that make fun of human weaknesses

verse: poetry

vocabulary: all of the words used or understood by a person or group

Index

Photo Credits

Cover illustration by Terry Paulhus
James L. Amos/CORBIS/MAGMA: pages 17, 22; Archive Photos: pages 3, 4;
Associated Press Photo: pages 3, 12; Copyright © 2002 Random House, Inc. Dr. Seuss
properties ™ copyright © 1937–2002 Dr. Seuss Enterprises, L.P. Used by permission
of Random House Children's Books, a division of Random House, Inc.: pages 26–27;
Corbis Corporation: page 21; Courtesy of the Connecticut Valley Historical Museum,
Springfield, Massachusetts: page 8; EyeWire, Inc.: page 13; From AND TO THINK THAT
I SAW IT ON MULBERRY STREET by Dr. Seuss, ™ copyright © Dr. Seuss Enterprises, L.P.
1937, renewed 1965. Used by permission of Random House Children's Books, a
division of Random House, Inc.: page 18; Map Resources: page 6; Ralph Morang:
page 9; PhotoDisc, Inc.: page 7; Photofest: pages 19, 20, 26, 28; Simple Oxford
Photo Library: page 11.